Your Guide To A Wealth Producing Home Based Business

UNKNOWN

YOUR GUIDE TO A WEALTH PRODUCING HOME BASED BUSINESS

Tom's Good 4U Products

2006

Your Guide To A Wealth Producing Home Based Business

TABLE OF CONTENTS

INTRODUCTION

You've always said to yourself, "When am I going to stop working for someone else? When am I going to make all my hard work pay off for me, instead of someone else?" Well, you're finally starting to do something about it! And you have chosen the perfect time! The explosion of the Internet population through the mid-1990's has leveled the playing field forever! It is now possible for the "little guy" to step up and make the big money! Wouldn't it be nice to someday walk into your boss's office and explain how you really don't need the job anymore? While this may sound like a wild fantasy to many people, it is becoming a reality to more people than you may realize! Now, let's set the record straight right here and now. I'm not about to make crazy promised with rags-to-riches fair tales. I'm also not going to recommend that you have that little chat with the boss tomorrow morning. Here's what I am going to tell you. The drive and ambition that prompted you to purchase this, couples with the information you are about to discover, will finally get you going in the direction of financial independence. Ask any financially independent person you can find (truly financially independent) and they'll all agree on one thing. You can't get rich working for someone else!

So, without further adieu, let's get the show on the road as they say. Or more appropriately for our purposes, let's keep the show at home. The following information has been organized in a manner that will assist you through the process of building a successful home-based business as smoothly as possible.

Be sure to give it your undivided attention, as it is not light reading material. Remember, this information, if used properly, could very well lead you to your goal of financial independence!

AT LAST!
A BUSINESS OF YOUR OWN!

At last, a business of your own! You've finally made a decision to move in the direction of financial freedom!

Given the technological advances in today's society, home-based businesses can do nothing but get stronger and stronger. With the personal computer and other high-tech gadgets finding their way into many homes, there may soon be very few reasons to leave the house for anything at all. After all, one would already be hard pressed to think of a single thing that is not readily available via the Internet.

Many people are turning to the on-line marketplace for the specialized information that will make their lives easier or richer. With the on-line population expected to exceed 100 million, the right information product, strategically marketed to the right consumer, a company can turn quite a profit.

Electronic marketing is just another way of communications. It is just another kind of marketing. Going on-line to sell products is just another method of reaching people. What makes it special is the speed and ease that you can reach your customers, and the cost effectiveness. Like anything else, though, you have to know what you are doing. Too many computer buffs are patting themselves on the back because they know how to access The internet, Bulletin Board Systems and post messages, upload and download files and more. They think that they can make money on-line because they know how run an add on Prodigy (TM) of CompuServe (TM), or one or many of the other major or many minor bulletin board systems. Quite frankly, that's the easy part. Now, you cannot make money on-line if you can't get on-line. But you cannot make money on-line just because you know how to get on-line.

Selling on-line is not altogether different from selling by mail. It's just a lot simpler.

There is no question that the only way to become financially independent is by owning your own business. yet the financial reasons are just the tip of the iceberg. The feeling of accomplishment you get from owning your own business can be incredibly satisfying. Ask anyone who has started their own business if they would trade their status as entrepreneur for their old nine-to-five grind. I'd be very surprised if you received a yes from any one of them. Even if their business has yet to turn a profit, the mere fact that they are in business for themselves is enough to keep them from missing their status as "employee".

You know how much you are making right now in your current job. You also probably have a good idea how much you'll be making in two, five or maybe even ten years from now. That is, if you continue working for someone else.

When you start your own company, however, the sky is the limit as far as earning potential. There's absolutely nothing wrong with keeping that nine-to-five job for as long as you want. Even after you have established a firm hold on the concept of making money on you own, you may prefer to keep right on working your regular job. There also is a good chance, however, that you may eventually find if only serves to weigh you down in your effort to make more money at home. Many companies started at home, by one person in their spare time, have flourished into major enterprises with revenues in the millions.

Just remember, nothing in this life is handed to you. You must be willing to make the commitment to work as hard as it takes to achieve the goals you set for yourself. If you would be content with an extra ten or twenty thousand dollars per year to supplement your income, then set that as your goal. Strive for it and achieve it. If you want to turn your business into a full time venture, you'll have to work even harder.

BUSINESS MATTERS TO ATTEND TO FIRST

For those of you just starting from scratch on your own, there are a few business matters that will need to be addressed. It's a good idea to take care of these matters relatively early in your business venture so you can concentrate on the heart of your business plan; that is, actually making money. I won't go into too much detail, but I would like to touch briefly on a few of the more important issues.

The first issue to concern yourself with is licensing and registration. There are many companies in existence today that have not taken the time to concern themselves with these "details" and therefore are not operating legally. Don't let your company become one of these "under the table" operations. you should strive to make your company become something you can be proud to own and operate and therefore keep it above board and legal. Not only are there many tax benefits when operating legally, but the feeling of clear conscience alone can be just as important.

Just think, you'll never have to worry about the tax man knocking on your door to collect his fair share (plus interest) of profits made over the last four years, or however long your company has been profitable. That reason alone can be enough to make you want to way on the up and up. Although it may seem easier now to just move on with your business and let the petty details fall by the wayside, believe me, it will be a lot harder later to keep this "under the table" business operating our of view of the powers that be.

So, the first step in the licensing and registration of your business is to call or stop by your local town hall and tell them you are interested in starting your own business. Ask them if you need to register this business and if there are any special requirements or licenses for a home-based business in your area. More than likely, you will not need any special permits or licenses to operate a business out of your home; however, you may need to register this business at a local and or state level. This is so that the public will be informed of your new business venture.

The next issue you may run into when checking into these business matters is zoning. Many of the zoning laws in the U.S. have been on the books for a long time and are largely ignored by home business owners. I do recommend, however, that you become aware of the zoning laws in your area, even though the type of business you'll be operating is usually not subject to zoning problems. Most of the zoning laws on the books are there to protect your neighbors' rights. Many officials realize that home businesses are on the increase everywhere and they tend to look the other way, unless requested to do otherwise by angry neighbors of a zoning violator.

The next business matter at hand is to choose a good name for your new business. You should put some thought into this, as it is the name that will represent your company for the life of its existence. At the time of registering your business you will be asked what your DBA (doing business as) name will be.

The firs rule of thumb in picking a name is to keep it fairly simple. Many people simply use their name followed by the word "Company" or "Associates". Keep in mind, you cannot use the word "Incorporated" or "Inc.", unless you are incorporated. Some people prefer to use their initials or a combination of initials that represent something to them. Whatever it is you decide to use, it should sound professional, since the name is often the first thing people will see about your company.

If you plan to use a name that describes the nature of your company, instead of one that uses your name, you'll need do to some checking. It is important to be sure that the name isn't already taken by someone else in your area. This search can be conducted by an attorney or can be done yourself. if you decide to do it yourself you should start by checking the Secretary of State business listing as well as your county business listing. Also, to be safe, you should check with the Federal Trademark Registry for any companies that do business in your area that may already be using this name. You don't want to use a name (knowingly or unknowingly) that is already being used and set yourself up for a possible lawsuit.

RULES & REGULATION

Since you are planning to start your own business, you need to be familiar with some of the rules that govern this industry. For all intents and purposes, this business would fall under the category of a mail-order business, especially if you plan to offer your information products in hard copy form. As long as you plan to run your business on the up and up, you should have no problems with any of the laws on the books.

Let's run through the major issues and see how they will pertain to you and your new business. Although there are many more regulations than what we will cover here, the thing to remember is this: Don't cheat anyone out of their hard earned money. When you run an honest business, you stand a much better chance at success. Here are some of the basics.

The Mail-order rule.

The Federal Trade Commission passes this rule in 1975. It is also known as the 30-day rule. It states that any order solicited through the male must be shipped within 30 days after receipt of payment. When you are soliciting orders for your product, you must believe that you can fill these orders within 30 days or specify the length of time it will actually take. Example: (Please allow five weeks for delivery.)

If you do not ship within 30 days or the specified time, you must notify the buyer of the delay and give them the option of canceling their order or accepting the delay. You must refund payment on any canceled orders promptly. This rule has been recently amended to include all orders taken over phone lines as well as through the mail. This rule is strictly enforced and should be taken very seriously.

Truth in advertising.

This can be summed up quite simply. It is unlawful to mislead the public in any way. You must describe the product being advertised clearly, without making any false claims, or omitting any important facts that the average person would need to know. Also, the word "new" should be avoided when advertising, since it only gives an accurate description of your product for the first six months of its existence. Also, the price of the item must be clearly stated in your advertisement. Be careful when stating prices. It is unlawful to claim that the price of your item was formerly higher than the current asking price unless you actually sold a substantial number of items at the higher price.

Any testimonials given must be genuine and authorized by the person who game them. You should be prepared to show proof of any testimonials, and they should be on an honest nature.

When giving a guarantee, it must give details of how it is carried out. Example: "If you are not completely satisfied with the product, return in in reasonably good condition within thirty days for a full refund." This clearly states the length of the guarantee and the conditions.

Keep in mind, these regulations have been put into place to protect the public. Unfortunately, since the early days of traditional mail-order there have been many companies that have operated in an illegal and deceitful manner. These companies have come and gone like the wind, and any companies started based on unlawful premised in the future are sure to meet the same fate. As you can clearly see, as long as you operate your mail-order operation honestly, you'll have no problem abiding by these rules and regulations.

START UP MATERIALS AND COSTS

Now that we have covered the necessary evils, let's start looking at some of the things you may need to purchase in the early stages of your business. One of the main reasons that a mail-order type of business is so attractive to the would-be entrepreneur, is its low initial start-up investment.

The list was made with the assumption that you already own a computer and all the hardware and software necessary to connect to the Internet and send and receive E-mail. Other than your monthly on-line charges, as you will see from the list, you really won't spend much, if anything!

Research material.

Anytime you take on a new venture, whether it be a business or a hobby, it's always a good idea to learn as much as you possibly can about this new interest of yours. This means you should read books, instructional literature, magazines and anything else related to your new area of interest. You can purchase these items or, better yet, make a trip to the local library. The libraries are filling up with information about on-line services!

Expected cost: $0-$100.00

Registration, licensing, permits.

You may need to do some form of registration to make your business legal. As suggested earlier, check with your local officials to find out exactly what is necessary in your area. don't make the mistake of waiting until it's too late. Do this relatively early in your business start-up period so you won't need to worry about it later.

Expected cost: $0-$200.00

Basic office supplies.

You certainly can spend a lot of money here, but don't. Just start with the very basics. Pens, pencils, paper, business size envelopes, and a good notebook should get you started in the beginning. You can purchase other larger office supplies on an "as needed" basis. Not included in this basic needs list is shipping supplies. These don't need to be purchased until you've actually sold your product. You should look into prices, though, to get a rough idea on the cost.

Expected cost: $0-$20.00

Business checking account.

You should open a business checking account sooner or later to keep all of your business transactions separate from your personal finances. It is important to have your business name on your checks to keep a professional image. You should open this account once you have chosen a name and registered your new business.

Expected cost: $0-$50.00

Office equipment.

Most people can probably get by without purchasing any office equipment at all. I started with an old card table with folding legs. The point is, don't go out and buy anything until you absolutely need it.

Expected cost: $0

Printer

If you don't already have a printer connected to your PC, you should think about getting one. You'll eventually need to print a letter to a customer or envelopes or even sales literature. Although you don't need to have one right away, consider the time it will save you in the long run. Anyway, here are a few things to consider before you purchase. There are basically three types available. Listed in order from low price range to high, they are on the dot matrix, the inkjet and the laser printer. Of course, the laser printer produces the best quality printing at the highest speeds; however you pay dearly for this performance. The low cost dot matrix type printers print at a decent speed; however, the quality is generally not as good as the other two. After much research, I would recommend an ink jet printer for someone just starting a home-based business. The prices are sensible and the printing quality is more than adequate. All three types come in black or color. In the average prices listed below for each type of printer, the lower cost reflects black and the higher cost reflects the color models.

Dot matrix printer: $100 to $300 Inkjet printer: $175 to %500 Laser printer: $325 to $2000 or more

Software

You should think about getting a good word processing or desktop publishing software on your computer. There are many available on the market ranging from $90 to $900. If you don't already have something similar, be sure the one you purchase has the ability to do labels and comes with free technical support. Another very helpful type of software to have is a mail list or address list program. You can keep a running customer list and keep track of product ship dates, amounts paid, E-mail addresses and other pertinent information. It is also very helpful when offering new products to existing customers.

The only thing I failed to mention in the list of startup items is something that you can't purchase…space. Of course you are going to need some space to set up a mini-office type of environment. A spare room, a basement or even a card table like I used should suffice in the start-up period of your business.

Once your business starts to grow, you will begin to require more space, so try to plan accordingly in the beginning, if at all possible. It's also a good idea to pick a place where you can get as much privacy as possible. I know from experience, however, that sometimes this is virtually impossible in some households. Anyway, try to pick a good place at the start, since it is very difficult to move everything once you have settled in.

That just about does it for start-up materials. You will probably come across a few things here and there, but there won't be many surprises now that you've read this fairly extensive start-up list. As you can see, you shouldn't need to purchase much to get started. Actually, most people won't need to buy a single thing! However, if you do need to get a few of the items listed, don't do it all at once! There's no reason to put yourself in the poorhouse before you have a chance to sell a single thing. Take your time in acquiring everything you decide to get.

INFORMATION IS PRICELESS…ALMOST!

The biggest, and by far the hardest decision when starting a mail-order type business has always been WHAT TO SELL! Once you finally made that decision, you were faced with the dilemma of acquiring your product! That's what makes this opportunity so unique. These two giant hurdles have already been bypasses. You are reading your first product right now!

As I've already explained, the best product in the world is without a doubt…INFORMATION. Not just any information, mind you, the information must be specialized and marketable. It must be specialized so that it can be marketed to a target audience, and it must be marketable in today's world to sell. That's where this manual comes in. The information contained in this manual is on the top of the list of most sought-after information in the world right now!

Now that you have your first specialized information product, it is time to learn a sound marketing strategy. A finished product is not of much value to you, unless you know how to successfully market and sell it.

The rest of this manual will teach you everything you need to know about the "meat" of your business plan. Keep in mind that you can't help but learn more and more about this incredible venture as you go along! Therefore, you will most likely adjust your business plan to suit your needs as you go. Anyway, here are the five basic steps you will be taking. After the brief outline, I will explain each step in detail.

1. Write a few good classified ads that are designed to get interested people to contact you.
2. Write a short yet powerful sales letter that you will e-mail to business opportunity seekers.
3. Utilize on-line marketing strategies. (Classified advertising, e-mailing lists and on-line advertising companies.)
4. Send your sales literature to your "prospects" via e-mail.
5. Fill orders you receive by mailing and or e-mailing your information product to your customer.

GETTING DOWN TO BUSINESS!

WRITING CLASSIFIED ADS

When writing your classifieds, keep in mind that your goal is to get interested people to identify themselves to you. You don't want to try to sell your product with the classified ads. People are not likely to pay more than a few dollars for something unless they have a lot of information about it. Your classifieds should be brief yet powerful. You simply want interested parties to contact you so you can send them more detailed information. This popular and very effective approach is known as "two step marketing".

Here's a good classified ad that utilizes the two step marketing strategy and works very nicely for an information product...

Strike It rich on the net! Don't let the opportunity of a lifetime pass you by! Learn how you can work at home in your spare time and make more money than you know what to do with! For more information, simply e-mail XXXX@YYY.ZZZ

This ad has all the key components of a great classified ad. First, there's the eye-catching headline. Then the first sentence gives a sense of urgency that people respond to. The next sentence tells them what they stand to gain if they respond. And the last sentence tells them exactly how to get more information.

WRITING YOUR SALES LITERATURE

To me, this is the fun part of the business. Creating good sales literature is more of an art form than anything else. you need to be able to change your mindset to that of the consumer. Keep this in mind as you create your sales letter. Remember, above all, your sales literature should be short and to the point. Here are a few guidelines to follow to get you started.

There are many key ingredients in a good sales letter. First and foremost, you must state clearly, exactly how your prospective customer would benefit from purchasing your product. In essence, tell them why they should purchase your product. Tell them how it could change their life for the better!

Additionally, it is important to tell the customer exactly what they will be buying. Tell them this is exactly what they are buying. It is important not to mislead people into thinking they are getting something different than they are.

Next, be sure to tell them exactly how much the product is. Include reasonable charges for shipping if necessary, but don't overcharge your customer.

Another important component in your sales literature is the guarantee. I highly recommend you offer some form of guarantee with every product you sell. The guarantee must be clear and concise as to its length and terms. Not only does a guarantee tell a prospective buyer that you are a reputable company, it will also increase your sales.

One thing about your sales literature that is very important is pricing of your product. You must understand the importance of "perceived value" where the customer feels they are getting their money's worth. In order to have any success at all, you must consider the pricing of your product very carefully. It is important to find the price that ideally suits your product. In order to do this, it may be necessary for you to do a little experimenting with your prices. It is a good idea to offer your product at a few different prices and constantly monitor what prices are most effective. You may find that something that sells well at sixteen dollars may not sell nearly as well at twenty dollars.

One more pricing issue that I would like to touch on is method of payment. Many mail-order companies deal strictly with cash, money orders and checks. This is the preferred method of payment by most customers as well. Many people are somewhat reluctant to use credit cards when dealing with unknown mail-order companies due to the increase in credit fraud. Additionally, credit card status is not always easy to obtain for new companies, unless you have a long-standing relationship with a bank. Checks are simply the most simple and preferred method of payment for both customers and mail-order companies alike.

Upon receiving personal checks, some companies prefer to deposit the check and wait a week before filling the order to be sure the check clears, however, I have not found this to be necessary. The very few checks that don't clear will usually go through when submitted a second time. Once again, it's all up to you.

The last important element of your sales literature that should not be overlooked is the order blank. It is a good idea to include this in any sales information that you send out.

An order blank should be designed with one purpose in mind. That purpose is to facilitate the ordering of your product. You want to make it as easy as possible for your prospective customer to complete. The order blank should contain blank lines for the customer to fill in all pertinent information, and only the pertinent information. Additionally, it should contain your company name and mailing address and the price of the product, including any additional shipping charges.

As far as the technical aspects of writing your sales literature, if you are a Windows user, you should save your sales letter as a text file (.txt). You can accomplish this by clicking the "accessories" icon, then the "notebook" icon and typing your letter there. This will allow you to keep a backup of your sales literature and also make it easier to send the information to your prospects using the simple cut-and-paste method. I'll give you more details on this simple procedure later.

ON-LINE MARKETING

On-line marketing is still very new and it is important to realize that this area of the on-line world is constantly growing and improving. Although you can spend a bundle of money when marketing on-line, this section will only cover the top four strategies for a small business on a limited budget.

They are (a) classified advertising, (b) e-mailing lists, (c) bulletin board services, and (d) on-line advertising companies. As your business continues to grow, you may want to explore other marketing tools such as getting your own web page complete with text and graphics. In the early stages of your business, however, you should find that one or more of the following strategies will work very well! I prefer to use free classifieds coupled with direct e-mailing. Remember, it's all up to you!

No matter what strategy you are using, it's important to understand that the biggest key to successful marketing is offering your product to the correct audience. Another way to describe this is "target marketing". I cannot emphasize the importance of this enough. In order for you to sell your product with any success whatsoever, you must concentrate your marketing efforts on the people that are most likely to buy it. Keep this in mind no matter which marketing strategy you utilize.

(a) Classified Advertising

You post your classified ads in the appropriate classified group (business, hobbies, books, etc.) and inform anyone who may read the classified that they can request more information by sending you an E-mail at your E-mail address. Once you receive the request, you simply E-mail the prospective customer with your sales literature. They can then print the details (including order form) and send for the product! When advertising your new information product, stick to the business areas on the Internet! Don't waste your time advertising your product in the "general merchandise" or "miscellaneous" sections! Concentrate solely on your target audience.

Before posting an ad, check out the business classified section at each site. Chances are, if the business section is fairly large, there must be a good reason. Most sites will also indicate their number of hits (number of on-line visitors to this particular site) as well, so you'll know how many customers may see your ad.

The number of locations that allow you to post classifieds is growing so fast that I can't begin to give you a reasonable estimate of how many there are. Most of them are completely free while others charge small fees. To find a large list of free classified areas on the internet, simply go to whatever search engine you use (Web Crawler, Info seek, Lycos, or any other) and enter the key words "free classifieds".

Upon entering a classified section, check into the "guidelines & regulations) area before posting. This is usually where you will find the rates, if they do charge. (Don't worry, they are required to tell you exactly how much you will be charged before they post your ad.)

Most sites require you to register with them before you can post your ad. This registration is also free unless otherwise stated. This is where you will usually find detailed directions for posting an ad. It is actually quite simple and only takes a few seconds. You simply type some information about yourself, then type your classified ad. Once all the information has been entered, you click on "post" or "submit" and you're done.

Remember, your ads should not try to sell your product! They are placed with the intention of getting interested people to respond to you so you can send your sales literature to them.

(b) E-mailing Lists

The next marketing strategy that is gaining popularity in the on-line world is called direct e-mail. This involves e-mailing your advertisements directly to a list of people who may be interested. This list is usually bought or rented from an e-mailing list broker. The costs vary widely depending on the broker used. This can be a very effective way to get your message out.

I was never an advocate of traditional mailing list strategies for two very big reasons. First of all, the cost of mailing to everyone on the list (at 37 cents a pop) usually offset any profits immediately. And secondly, a lot of this mail was considered junk mail and was never even opened!

Direct e-mail does not have these downfalls. First of all, sending e-mail is free, saving you hundreds or thousands of dollars in postage. And secondly, the e-mail sits at the person's mailbox until it is opened. These two factors couples with the high number of people you can reach in a very short amount of time warrants giving this dynamic new marketing strategy a try!

Remember, don't try to sell your products with the first contact. Simply offer the opportunity to receive "free details" by replying to the ad. Then e-mail your sales letter to these new prospects.

Until very recently, this marketing strategy had been highly frowned upon by a large segment of the on-line population. Although it is becoming more and more accepted as the net goes commercial, don't be disturbed by an occasional "flaming". This is the Internet term for a rude, harsh and often disgusting reply to unsolicited e-mail. Accept it as part of the on-line culture and move on with your business.

You can avoid a lot of flaming by seeking out a list of "opportunity seekers only". You can also keep it to a minimum by sending only short unsolicited messages and offering everyone an option to be removed from your list. Eventually, everyone will accept the inevitable commercialization of the Internet.

(c) Bulletin Board Services and News-groups

Another way to market products is via Bulletin Board Services and News-groups. These are set up for people with similar interests. Once you find your area of interest (i.e.: business opportunities), you can join them either for free or by registering with the "SYSOP" (person that runs a BBS) and paying a small fee.

Once you join a BBS or Newsgroup you then have the ability to post messages. A typical message posting in a business area would be similar to a classified ad. It would contain your offer and your e-mail address to allow people to request more information (your sales literature).

Some news-groups and BBS's allow members to download as well as upload files or programs for free. A download means transferring files to your computer. An example of something you would download would be shareware. Shareware is software that you can try out for free. If you like it, you are expected to register it with it's creator by paying a nominal fee. An upload means transferring files (such as information to attract interest in your product) to a BBS. These uploaded files are then downloaded by other PC users. This is a good way to get free exposure to your product.

When you join one of these groups, it's a good idea to just observe for a little while. This way you can get a feel for the way users do things in that particular group. This is a good way to avoid breaching the group regulations or "netiquette".

(d) On-line Marketing Companies

Another way to get your message out is to hire someone else to do it for you. All of these companies charge some type of fee to get your message across to potential customers.

There are already a number of companies offering on-line marketing strategies of one type or another. One example of another marketing strategy being utilized is direct e-mail magazines and newsletters. The companies that send these e-mail magazines offer paid advertising to small business owners for a relatively small fee. The fees are based on the size of ad as well as the circulation or number of e-mail addresses that receive the issue.

To find some of these companies and get more information, simply use whatever search engine you use to search the Internet (WebCrawler, Info seek, etc.). Search on the words "Internet marketing" or "business marketing". You'll get a nice long list to check out. Send an e-mail to the ones that sound the best and they will be more than happy to e-mail you some free details.

As I stated earlier, the world of on-line marketing is still in relative infancy. This means that a smart entrepreneur will stay very open-minded and receptive to new marketing strategies as they are being introduced. The businesses that make the most money will be the ones that keep a keen eye out for the potential winning strategies.

E-MAILING YOUR SALES MESSAGE

Once you have some e-mail addresses to send your sales letter to, you need to be able to do it quickly and efficiently. This may take a little practice at first.

If you've gotten this far along in this venture, you obviously know how to use e-mail. I also realize that all e-mail packages operate differently. However, whether you use AOL, Genie, Netcom or any other Internet service provider, if you run Windows you can utilize the basic "cut and paste" feature to simplify your e-mailing.

First of all, it's a good idea to write your sales letter in the Notebook application of Windows. I won't go into the details of how to do this since most Windows users will have no problem with it. (If you aren't sure how, look in your Windows book.) Once you complete your letter, you simply highlight all text and hold down "CTRL" and press "C". This stores the text in memory until you are ready to paste it.

Now you can go into your e-mail feature and click your cursor into the box where you would start typing your e-mail message. Instead of typing your message, you simply hold down "CTRL" and press "V". This will paste the entire letter exactly where you want it. You can do this "CTRL" "V" over and over until you replace what is in memory with something new by highlighting new text and pressing "CTRL" "C" again.

Keep in mind, if you have an e-mail list to mail to, you can also use this "cut and paste" method to paste multiple addresses and send to them all at once.

FILLING ORDERS

The last stop in completing a sale is the actual fulfillment of the order. As with every other aspect of your business, there are many options to consider when filling orders. The best advice I can give is to ship the product within a week of receiving an order. (Don't forget the 30 Day Rule.)

As far as the order-filling itself goes, there will be basically two methods. The first is (a) via regular mail and the second is (b) via E-mail. It's up to you to decide which method you will use. I prefer to offer both since they are both so simple to do.

If you plan to offer this manual via regular mail, obviously you'll need to get some copies printed. The best thing to do is bring it to one of the many quick print and copy centers that are cropping up all over the place. If they don't do it themselves; they should be able to get good copies printed up for less than 5 bucks per copy, including cover. There are a variety of methods, so shop around and get the best price!

(a) When mailing your product, the most important topic to cover is the addressing of your packages. I highly recommend a label program if you have a printer. Not only does this allow you to keep your customer list on computer, it also makes for much easier addressing of envelopes. If you don't have the software yet, just be sure that all packages are addressed clearly and legibly. Also make an effort to include all key components of the mailing address including apartment number (if applicable) and zip code. Be sure to include a return address on every outgoing package in case it can't be delivered.

Postage is the next thing to consider. If you are charging your customer for shipping and handling, don't gouge your customers. There are many mail-order companies "squeezing" a few extra dollars out of their customers by charging inflated shipping and handling charges. This unethical behavior is exactly the type of conduct that gives mail-order a bad name.

(b) The second method of filling orders is by using E-mail. E-mailing your product is even easier than using regular mail. (Not to mention the zero cost factor.) Be sure your e-mail program let's you attach files before you offer this method of delivery. (Almost all do by now.) You simply compose an e-mail in the regular fashion and then choose "attach file" before sending. Once you choose "attach file" you will be prompted to choose a file for your computer. All you do next is select the text file (.txt) you want to send and then send it. If you can't find the file on your computer, look in the "download" area of your on-line software directory. This is usually where all files you receive via your modem are stored.

One very important issue to consider, when filling orders via E-Mail, is that there are many different E-mail programs in use. Some will only accept files up to a certain size. If the file is too large (as HOME-BASED! txt is in some instances) the file will automatically be encoded to ease transmission. The process of converting the file back to a readable format may be a little beyond the realm of knowledge for many computer users. Additionally, some E-mail programs require separate programs to achieve this conversion. For this reason, it is a good idea to offer the .txt version on a floppy disk via regular mail. This actually serves a few purposes. In addition to saving the headache of receiving the attachment properly, it provides them with a backup copy, and also simplifies things when they are ready to send the manual as an attachment.

REINVEST IN YOURSELF

The last point I would like to make involves growth. Simply put, as profits increase, you should continue to re-invest these profits. This continued reinvesting of profits is necessary to insure continued growth of your business, and in turn, the continued increasing profits that come with it.

Needless to say, there are many ways to reinvest profits. One of the best ways is to continually evaluate and upgrade the scope of your marketing. This usually means spending more on your advertising and other marketing techniques. You may want to consider contacting some Internet advertising agencies for fresh ideas.

Another key factor to growing in your business is to continually add new products and sales literature. (Also continue to enhance existing literature.) You should always remember that your own customer base is the best place to introduce new products. Consider sending an e-mail message to all of your existing customers to offer new information products that you purchase or develop yourself.

There are lots of other ways to reinvest profits. Upgrading office equipment for example, may be near the top of your list. Whatever your particular company needs are, keep in mind that your primary objective when reinvesting profits should be to create more sales. If purchasing new office equipment will aid you in producing better quality products and sales literature, then it may very well be necessary. On the other hand, if your products are selling well already, you may benefit the most by simply placing more classifieds. The beauty of it is the fact that it's your decision and no one else's.

IT'S ALL UP TO YOU TO GET STARTED

You now have everything you need to get your home business started and shifted into high gear immediately! Not only do you possess the knowledge, you have the ideal product as well!

So what are you waiting for? Are you worried you won't succeed? Why not look at it like this. If you try to succeed in your own business and fail, the most you will lose is a little money. After all, you don't have to risk your life savings when starting this business. The knowledge alone, that you will gain from starting your own business will outweigh any financial loss by far.

You must also keep in mind that success can be a difficult thing to sneak up on. Perseverance is a major asset to anyone starting their own business. After all, failure, as well as success is a part of life. As the old saying goes, if at first you don't succeed, try, try again. This saying wouldn't be so popular if everyone succeeded the very first time they attempted anything. Remember, all progress involves some form of risk.

Now that you know the worst that can happen (and it isn't all that bad, is it?) let's concentrate on the best case scenario! If you succeed, and more than 75% of all new entrepreneurs do, you will no longer have to rely on others for your income! You'll be able to work the hours YOU want to work, right in your own home! So what are you waiting for? YOU CAN DO IT! Have faith in yourself and go for it!

Follow through and I know that you will be the successful business owner you deserve to be…!

Checklist
For mail order success
The company name

1. Select a short, friendly, informal, easy-to-remember company name.

2. Your personal name is acceptable, but add "Co.", "Gifts", etc.

3. Home address or post office box makes no appreciable difference.

Starting supplies

4. Neatly printed letterheads and envelopes.

5. A typewriter or computer—or the availability of one is a must.

6. Parcel post shipping labels.

7. Avoid purchasing expensive office equipment of supplies until absolutely needed for more efficient operation—and capital permits.

Starting capital

8. To purchase above starting supplies.

9. To pay for two or three publication ads to test your offer.

10. Or, to pay rental for a minimum of 1,000 names for a direct mail program, plus postage costs.

11. To pay for preparation and layout of a display ad.

12. To pay for art work and typesetting of circular.

13. To pay for additional or continuing promotions if initial results are encouraging.

14. Costs to cover promotion expenses if further testing is required.

15. Extra capital to allow for unforeseen and unexpected expenses.

The Product

Select a product that:

16. Is new, unusual and, if possible, exclusively yours

17. Is of good quality and fairly priced.

18. Fills a definite need for a wide and ready market.

19. Offers strong appeal to the prospect.

20. Is not commonly sold in retail stores.

21. Cannot be bought elsewhere or only from limited sources.

22. You can control its production or distribution.

23. Is not expensive to make or produce; can be bought at low price.

24. Interests a large percentage of the market.

25. Is not seasonable (except Christmas); can be sold year round.

26. Lightweight; not fragile; safe and inexpensive to ship.

27. Will be used up or consumed and must be reordered periodically.

Locating a suitable mail order item:

28. Look through mail order sections or magazines to check types of products successful mail order dealers offer.

29. Inquire of local manufacturers and Chamber of Commerce.

30. Attend trade shows (with gift, jewelry, household themes, etc.).

31. Contact appropriate manufacturers listed in Thomas Register, available at Public Libraries.

32. Watch for new product listings in trade journals and magazines.

33. Check out close-outs, surplus and overstock offers.

34. Contact mail order supply sources.

35. Design, develop, manufacture of publish your own product.

The line

36. Develop or acquire other items to tie in with your main product.

37. Present follow-up offers to customers and prospects.

38. Promote succession of products appealing to the same trade.

39. Sell such services as personalization, consultation, etc., if such services are adaptable to your line.

The advertising copy

40. Use attention-getting, bold headline copy in ads.

41. illustrate the product if space permits: explain how it is used.

42. Write copy in brief, bouncy, down-to-earth style.

43. Avoid any overly-clever, tricky phrases or expressions.

44. Be sincere; don't exaggerate.

45. Describe the product clearly and fully.

46. Stress the "YOU" approach; tell how the offer will benefit him.

47. Avoid excessive talking about yourself or your company.

48. Strive for conviction and sincerity—be believable.

49. Instill confidence; make the prospect feel you are honest.

50. Stir him into action to order your product.

51. Give specific directions for ordering.

52. Provide a guarantee or satisfaction or money back.

53. Tailor the ad/literature to fit the prospect you want to reach.

Testing your offer

54. If the capital permits, test more than one magazine.

55. Test more than one ad, each in a different publication.

56. Try split runs if the magazine offers regional or sectional issues.

57. Continue a successful ad without change until its pull drops to break-even point.

58. Don't rush to change an ad that is pulling well; experiment slowly.

59. Test only one change at a time: size of ad—copy—different appeal—new headline—another illustration—new price.

60. Use short testimonials if space permits.

61. Offer a bonus—something free or at a reduced price.

62. Key each ad or mailing to determine where results were derived.

63. Keep accurate records of returns from each promotion.

Sales literature

64. Usually consists of sales letter, descriptive circular or folder, order form, return envelope. (Some offers may be effectively sold by only a sales letter.)

65. Effective sales letter must create AIDA—Attention, Interest, Desire, Action.

66. The circular should fully illustrate or describe the product. It must provide more detailed information about the product—its uses, benefits, advantages and other special appeals.

67. Return envelope is an essential part of sales literature to make it convenient for the customer to mail the order.

68. Mailing sales offers by first-class mail vs third-class mail usually shows no appreciable difference in results.

69. Mailing envelope can feature an attractive design or teaser message to induce the recipient to open and read the offer.

The product supplier

70. Develop or produce your own mail order item, if possible.

71. Try to arrange exclusive mail-order rights with the supplier.

72. Establish supply sources close to home to save delivery time and shipping costs.

73. Seek lowest price if item is offered by two or more suppliers.

74. Order larger quantities, if you can afford such purchases, to get lower prices or greater discounts.

75. Ensure the supplier is reliable and will provide the merchandise you plan to promote: that he will ship orders promptly.

76. Consider only products which allow an adequate profit margin. (at least a 3 to 1 profit mark-up on lower-priced items).

77. Consider a supplier who is willing to "drop-ship" your orders directly to your customers—seek at least a 50% discount.

The selling price

78. Price merchandise fairly: give customers their money's worth.

79. Include postage or shipping costs in selling price.

80. Use round numbers ($3.00, $5.00, etc.) for lower-priced items to make it convenient for customers to remit payment.

81. Allow for all costs in marking up prices—postage, overhead, packing, allowances for non-deliveries, refunds, bad checks.

82. Be certain to allow yourself an adequate mark-up to assure profit.

83. Test different prices to determine which selling price brings in the greatest amount of profit.

Advertising

84. Don't attempt to start unless you can afford at least two or three ads; or pay for a direct mailing to at least 1,000 names.

85. Plan to advertise consistently.

86. Use ad space relative to sale price, i.e., use small-size ads for low-priced items and larger ads for more expensive items.

87. Items priced over $3.00 usually do not sell as profitably through classified ads.

88. In space ads, offer products in the $3.00 to $10.00 price range.

89. It is usually better to advertise for inquiries if an item sells for $10.00 or more.

90. Two small ads will generally produce more business than one ad twice as large.

91. Keep repeating ads as long as they continue to be profitable.

92. Don't waste unnecessary space; advertising is expensive.

93. Don't expect to make a killing from one ad or mailing. Consistent advertising is the key to mail order success.

The media

94. Newspapers with mail order sections bring quick returns and are acceptable for initial test. Results are not usually as good as from magazine ads for long-range pull.

95. Use only publications with the type of readership who will react favorably to your type of product or offer.

96. Unsold inquirers should be followed up with special inducements or with new offers.

97. Rent names only from reliable brokers or mail order sources.

98. Use only lists of people who are logical prospects for your offer.

99. Compile a mailing list from your own inquirers and customers.

100. Offer your names to list brokers; this is a good source for extra income.

101. Advertise in publications which feature large mail order sections; place ads in the same issues or sections in which your competitors advertise.

The advertising agency

102. Select an advertising agency experience in mail order.

103. Check their credentials; current accounts; successful promotions.

104. Don't use agencies which represent direct competitors.

105. Expect to pay in advance for ad placements and other services until credit terms are established.

106. Advertising agencies are not infallible. Forgive an honest mistake. Give the agency at least a second chance.

107. Expect to pay for preparation of display ads, copy layout, and other services you authorize. Classified ad copy will be prepared without any cost to you.

108. Extend full cooperation; go along with their recommendations.

109. If your advertising budget is substantial, consider setting up your own advertising agency—thereby saving 15% commission, plus a 2% discount in many instances.

Shipments

110. Fill and ship orders promptly. Mail order buyers get edgy with delays.

111. use plain but sturdy packing to ship orders.

112. Ship via parcel post or U.P.S., whichever is cheaper.

113. Use neatly printed shipping labels.

114. Address labels with typewriter; not by hand unless indelible ink is used and address printed.

115. Specify "Return Guaranteed" on labels or package.

Terms of payment

116. Accept personal checks; very few bounce.

117. Avoid C.O.D.'s unless you receive sufficient down payment to assure you have collected enough to cover the costs of the return, plus costs of handling and repacking the merchandise.

118. Don't offer to sell on credit or time payments unless item is high-priced and you can afford to carry credit accounts.

The customer

119. Consider the customer your greatest asset. Acknowledge that he is always right, even when he isn't.

120. Handle complaints promptly; write courteous explanation.

121. Offer replacement if product is broken or damaged.

122. Issue immediate refunds; adjust over payments promptly.

123. Promote new or other products to your customer list. No other class of prospect will be as responsive.

124. Work your customer list until it no longer proves profitable.

You

125. You, mainly, control the destiny of your mail order business.

126. Be energetic; devote as much time as you can spare to advance your enterprise to a more profitable future.

127. Be determined to make your mail order business a huge success.

128. Learn as much as you can about mail order techniques.

129. Be original; exclusive.

130. Don't copy anyone; copy only successful methods and techniques; always strive to improve on them.

131. Keep searching diligently for new, "exclusive" products.

132. Don't become disappointed by a slow start, or discouraged by a failure or two along the way.

133. Always perform professionally; an amateur does not get paid for his services.

134. Build your own financial pyramid; reinvest profits into productive programs that may mushroom your profits steadily.

135. Avoid being an easy mark for "get-rich-quick" schemes; start and operate your business on sound principles.

136. Refer to this handy checklist periodically—remind yourself to follow only accepted guidelines that control the safe operation of a mail order business.

HOW TO BUILD A $1,000 A WEEK MAIL ORDER BOOK BUSINESS

Among the most popular of all products sold by mail are books. In fact, more books are sold by mail than through retail book stores. Not all books are suitable for mail selling, but those which fill an important need can become the foundation of a highly successful and profitable business.

SUBJECTS TO CHOOSE AND AVOID

Regardless of your personal reading taste, most books are taboo for selling by mail, so let's examine these first. To be avoided are technical or scholarly books, primarily because they are readily found in local book stores and public libraries.

The same can be said about novels, history and biographies. Poetry books, although very popular, do not make mail order products. All of these subjects, in addition to their availability locally, are sold by major book clubs, so you would be competing directly with them.

The best subjects are books that provide help, ideas, inspiration and information, or those that contain solutions to problems relating to economic conditions and social lifestyles. Specifically, this includes "how-to" subjects, either in the titles or as suggested by the contents.

SUBJECTS MUST APPEAL TO HUMAN DESIRES

Virtually all successful mail order books offer help or ideas in one or more of the following classifications:

Health, Money, Time, Jobs, Careers, Self Assurance, Popularity, Fame, Security, Pleasure, Business

That's what people want. If you have a book (or set of books) that will show people how to make more MONEY, get a better JOB, become SELF-ASSURED, gain better HEALTH, put more PLEASURE into their lives, increase their PUPULARITY, Manage their TIME more wisely, become FAMOUS, increase their SECURITY, or put more profits into BUSINESS——then, you will have something that can be classified as a "winner."

PLAN TO SPECIALIZE

Right from the beginning, keep this thought in mind: You can't be all things to all people. Attempting to do so will dilute your efforts and increase your costs of doing business. The person who is seeking a better job is NOT necessarily interested in gaining better health or pleasure. The buyer of a book on time management may not be interested in becoming more popular. So, your first priority should be to determine the TYPE of subjects or books you want to handle, then target your advertising to that classification. Or, do it in reverse. Decide the type of person you would like to have as your customer, then select the category of books he/she would be interested in buying.

WHERE TO FIND BOOKS TO SELL

This will seem strange, but the worst suppliers of books for mail order selling are the major publishers. True, they may have some good titles, but the discounts they offer are much too low, usually 33% to 40% off retail.

You need a bare minimum of 50% discount on all books that you sell, and if you can get 60 to 70% that's even better. If you have sufficient capital to invest in your book business, contact a few book remainder companies.

Publishers Central Bureau, One Champion Ave., Avenel NJ 07131

Book Sales, Inc., 110 Enterprise Ave., Secaucus, NJ 07097

Overstock Book Co., 120 Secatogue Ave., Farmingdale, NY 11735

S & L Sales Company, PO Box 2067, Industrial Boulevard, Waycross, GA 31502

The above are prominent companies at the time of this writing, but circumstances are constantly changing. Check your local library for current addresses.

If you are not familiar with the book remainder business, this is how they generally operate:

Major publishers will carry a book for six months to a year, then if it is not moving profitably they will sell all remaining copies to one of these companies (often at 5 cents on the dollar) who, in turn, sells it to retail book sellers. It's important to point out that, just because a particular book title didn't sell well in bookstores does not necessarily mean it's a lemon. It usually means that no effort was made to promote it other than place it on the shelves in stores. With the right kind of advertising and thoughtful promotional methods, such books could become very profitable to an alert mail order bookseller.

Remainder books can often be purchased at up to 90% off retail, giving you a very high markup. But there are two main drawbacks in dealing with book remainder or overstock companies.

First, you have to pay cash up front for the books you purchase, and these companies normally do not offer return privileges. Thus, if a company has a total of 20,000 copies of a single title and you buy 1,000 at 50 cents each, it's a great buy, especially if you can retail the book for $10 or $12…but it's still a $500 investment. If the book doesn't sell, you're out the original cost of books, plus all advertising and printing of sales literature that you have created for it.

Second, if you hit on a good title that proves to be hot, and you sell out your first thousand copies, you'll want to go back for the remaining 19,000…but in the meantime the company might have already sold them to someone else.

The bottom line on this subject is that dealing with remainder houses is best left until you have experience in choosing and selling books before making a major investment in remainders.

SELF-PUBLISHERS OFFER GREAT OPPORTUNITIES

There are thousands of small, independent publishers in the USA and Canada, usually referred to as self-publishers, meaning these people have written a book on a subject they know well, then published it themselves.

Some of these self-publishers sell their books retail only, directly to their selected market, but many of them also want dealers to help market their books, and they offer excellent wholesale prices.

The small publishing field is wide and diversified, ranging from the individual who writes from a home or office to a small company employing only two or three key persons. The material they publish is equally diverse, from small booklets of 12 pages to giant volumes of several hundred pages. Subjects range from coin collecting to business management; from computer operation to various business opportunities and various money-making ideas.

Some of this material is excellent, but much of it is also poorly written and printed, resulting in amateurish attempts at publishing. To work with these publishers, you'll simply have to search out and evaluate each publisher and their titles.

HOW AND WHERE TO FIND THEM

Check the many tabloid mail order papers and magazines for their ads. Some of these trade journals also publish New Products departments in which they feature new books and booklets on the market.

You'll also find a column, "Stew's Reviews", published in **"JACKPOT"** TM National Shopper, which highlights many of the latest books, manuals, booklets, and other material being written and published.

When you first encounter some of these publishers, don't be dissuaded by the physical size of some of these publications. A great many are not really books at all, but are merely booklets, but your interest should be centered on content, for this is what you will be selling and your customers will be buying. People don't buy a book, they buy information, ideas, help, guidance, instruction and solutions to a wide range of problems. Naturally, you should be concerned with neatness in presentation, cover design, printing quality, layout and graphics, and each book or booklet should be well written and offer useable information.

Consider this: If someone has spend 20 to 40 years perfecting a craft or project that has proven to be a profitable business idea, and has now put this information in a book or booklet that others can use to accomplish the same as the authors, would this information not be worth $15 or more?

Of course it would. That's why such books and booklets are so popular with mail order booksellers, and why they're so profitable. The smaller publisher does not have a high overhead as the large publishing houses, so they can well afford to give a deeper discount to dealers. A $15 retail booklet, for example, can often be purchased in wholesale lots of a dozen for about $5 or $6 each, and most of these publishers will also sell on a drop ship arrangement, so the dealer has no investment in the books to be sold.

If you are not familiar with the drop ship term, it will simply means that you advertise to get orders for the books you sell, then deduct your commission and send the balance with your customer's name and address to the publisher, and he fills the order for you. The normal commission on a drop ship arrangement is 50% of retail.

To learn more about mail order and selling books by mail, you should read "**JACKPOT**"TM National Shopper. Each issue is loaded with valuable ideas, information, suppliers and contacts. To receive a current issue send $2.50 to: "**JACKPOT**"TM, PO Box 6547, Jacksonville, FL 32110 and request a copy of the magazine.

ADVERTISING AND PROMOTION

Your best advertising method will be in the classified sections of appropriate magazines. Use the heading that most clearly describes your book subject. Don't try to get direct orders, but ask only for names and addressees, then send inquiries information via a sales letter, descriptive circular, order form and return address envelope. In most cases the publisher of the books you sell will furnish you with a copy of the circular which he has printed. Sales letters, however, are rarely available from publishers so you will have to write your own or hire a professional copywriter, but you really do need a letter to accompany a circular.

Your offer should be priced at least $20. If your proposed book is only $5 or $10, it will not pay to advertise for inquiries. In such case, try to locate a companion book or booklet that you can combine with the primary title so it will boost your retail price to at least $20 or more.

HOW MUCH CAN YOU MAKE AS A BOOK SELLER?

If you have a good offer, priced at least $20, and if you have good printed sales materials to send to inquiries, you should be able to AT LEAST TRIPLE the cost of each ad you run. A $100 ad should, therefore produce $300 in sales.

If you can NET $50 profit from each ad and you run the same ad in 20 magazines, each producing the same $50 net, this will give you $1000 a month, assuming each magazine is published monthly. But using this example as a base, it means $12,000 annually…from your FIRST OFFER.

>From every 1000 inquiries you receive you will probably convert only about 15% into customers, leaving 850 inquiries who do not order. you can then follow up these inquiries by sending additional book offers three or four times a year to convert more of them into customers. Also, continue mailing to those who purchase your books from you. These customers will stick with you and continue to buy as long as you keep mailing to them. Just be sure your offer is something they are interested in.

Continue to search out and add more books to your growing line, eventually producing them into your own catalog. The major profits will continue to come as long as you continue to mail to your growing customer and inquiry lists.

www.ingramcontent.com/pod-product-compliance
Lightning Source LLC
Chambersburg PA
CBHW081230170526
45165CB00009B/3019